Revised and Updated

Uniquely
Ohio

Marcia Schonberg

Heinemann Library
Chicago, Illinois

www.heinemannraintree.com
Visit our website to find out
more information about
Heinemann-Raintree books.

To order:

☎ Phone 888-454-2279

💻 Visit www.heinemannraintree.com
to browse our catalog and order online.

Edited by Megan Cotugno
Designed by Ryan Frieson, Kim Miracle, Betsy Wernert
Photo research by Tracy Cummins
Originated by Heinemann Library
Printed in China by Leo Paper Products Ltd.

13 12 11 10 09
10 9 8 7 6 5 4 3 2 1

New edition ISBNs: 978-1-4329-2574-1 (hardcover)
978-1-4329-2581-9 (paperback)

Library of Congress Cataloging-in-Publication Data
Schonberg, Marcia.
  Uniquely Ohio / Marcia Schonberg.
    v. cm. -- (Heinemann state studies)
Includes bibliographical references and index.
Contents: Uniquely Ohio -- State Symbols -- State Motto
-- State Quarter -- State Ships -- Agriculture and Festivals
-- Ohio's Music -- State Flag -- State Seal -- Local and State
Government -- Mother of Presidents -- Bridges -- Foods --
Sports Teams and Legends -- Sights and
Sounds of Ohio -- Stamps of Ohio.
  ISBN 1-4034-0670-7 -- ISBN 1-4034-2693-7 (pbk.)
  1. Ohio--Juvenile literature. [1. Ohio.] I. Title. II. Series.
  F491.3.S37 2003
  977.1--dc21
                    2002154208

Acknowledgments

The author and publishers are grateful to the following for
permission to reproduce copyright material: **pp. 5, 45** maps.
com/Heinemann Library; **p. 6** onemileup.com; **pp. 6-7, 16,
20-21, 24, 28-29** Robert Lifson/Heinemann Library; **pp.
8T, 18T, 20, 22** Tom Uhlman; **p. 8B** Jeremy Woodhouse/
PhotoDisc/Getty Images; **pp. 9, 37B, 38, 43T** Jim Baron/The
Image Finders; **p. 10T** Tom McHugh/Photo Researchers,
Inc.; **p. 10B** Scott Camazine/Photo Researchers, Inc.; **p. 11T**
Joe McDonald/Corbis; **p. 11B** United States Department
of the Treasury; **p. 12** Ohio Governors Office; **p. 14** Ohio
Governors Office; **p. 15** The Supreme Court of Ohio; **p. 17**
Stewart Halfacre/City of Dayton; **p. 18B** Jeff Greenberg/Visuals
Unlimited; **p. 21** courtesy Columbus Symphony Orchestra;
pp. 23, 40B Jeff Greenberg/The Image Works; **p. 25** Richard
Hamilton Smith/AgStockUSA; **p. 26** courtesy Skyline Chili;
p. 28 North Wind Picture Archives; **p. 30** Paul Sancya/AP
photo; **p. 31** Wilson Sporting Goods; **p. 32** Reuters NewMedia
Inc./Corbis; **p. 33** Carl A. Stimac/The Image Finders; **p. 34**
courtesy General Mills; **p. 35** Honda of America Mfg., Inc.;
p. 36 UPPA/Photoshot; **p. 37T** Michael Philip Manheim/The
Image Finders; **p. 39** Al Behrman/AP Wide World Photos; **p.
40T** Layne Kennedy/Corbis; **p. 41** Richard A. Cooke/Corbis; **p.
42** Richard Cummins/SuperStock; **p. 43B** Charles E. Rotkin/
Corbis; **p. 44** Bettmann/Corbis; Steve Raymer/Corbis

Cover photograph of the World's Largest Basket in
Frazeysburg, Ohio, reproduced with permission of ©Jeff
Greenberg/age footstock.

Every effort has been made to contact copyright holders of
any material reproduced in this book. Any omissions will
be rectified in subsequent printings if notice is given to the
publisher.

All the Internet addresses (URLs) given in this book were valid
at the time of going to press. However, due to the dynamic
nature of the Internet, some addresses may have changed, or
sites may have changed or ceased to exist since publication.
While the author and Publishers regret any inconvenience this
may cause readers, no responsibility for any such changes can
be accepted by either the author or the Publishers.

Contents

Some words are shown in bold, **like this**. You can find out what they mean by looking in the glossary.

Uniquely Ohio

Ohio is tucked between Lake Erie and the Ohio River, in the U.S. Midwest. This geographic location is one of the things that has helped to make Ohio unique. Something that is unique has special characteristics or features that are not usually found anywhere else. Ohio's location on Lake Erie and the Ohio River has enabled the state to become one of the nation's leading manufacturing centers.

Ohio, the seventeenth state to join the United States, has many other unique and special features, too. Ohio is the birthplace of seven U.S. presidents—more than any other state except Virginia, which has eight. Dayton, Ohio, boasts the world's oldest and largest military museum. The first full-time car service station opened in 1899 in Ohio. It is also the only state that has a town name starting with every letter of the alphabet. Towns starting with *Q*, *X*, and *Z* are uncommon. However, Ohio has Quaker City, Quincy, Xenia, Zaleski, and Zanesville. Read on to discover even more interesting and unique aspects of Ohio.

Unique Facts About Ohio

- First **interracial/coeducational** college: Oberlin College, Oberlin, 1833

- Vulcanized rubber invented: Charles Goodyear, Akron, 1839

- First professional baseball team: Cincinnati Red Stockings, Cincinnati, 1869

- First public weather forecast released: Cleveland Abbe, Cincinnati, 1869

- First electrically lighted city: Cleveland, 1880

- First automobile built: John Lambert, Ohio City, 1891

- Electric traffic signal lights invented: James Hoge, Cleveland, 1914

- Teflon invented: Roy Plunkett, New Carlisle, 1938

Things to See in Ohio

Ohio State Symbols

State Flag

Ohio adopted its state flag in 1902. Ohio's flag is the only U.S. state flag with a unique triangular shape. The shape as well as the blue triangle symbolizes Ohio's hills and valleys. The flag's stripes stand for its roads and waterways. The 17 stars on the flag stand for the 17 states at the time of Ohio's statehood in 1803. The red center of the *O* stands for the first letter in "Ohio" and has the same shape as a buckeye nut, which is common in the state.

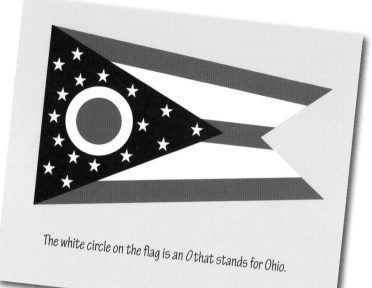

The white circle on the flag is an O that stands for Ohio.

State Seal

The sun in the seal has 13 rays, one for each of the Thirteen Colonies.

Ohio adopted its current seal in 1996. The bunch of 17 arrows on the left stands for Ohio's entry into the United States as the 17th state. The sun rises over the **Allegheny Mountains**—one of which is Mount Logan in Ross County. The sun's rays shine over Ohio—the first state in the **Northwest Territory**. The Scioto River flows on the left, next to a lush farm field that symbolizes Ohio's fertile croplands.

State Song: "Beautiful Ohio"

"Beautiful Ohio" became Ohio's official state song in 1969.

Drifting with the current down a moonlit stream
While above the heavens in their glory gleam
And the stars on high, twinkle in the sky
Seeming in a paradise of love divine
Dreaming of a pair of eyes that looked in mine
Beautiful Ohio, in dreams again I see
Visions of what used to be

The song was not about the state itself. Instead, it described a love story that took place on the Ohio River. In 1989 Ohio lawmakers voted to change the words to "Beautiful Ohio." They wanted words that described their state. A Youngstown lawyer named Wilbert McBride wrote these new words:

I sailed away;
Wandered afar;
Crossed the mighty restless sea;
Looked for where I ought to be.
Cities so grand, mountains above,
Led to this land I love.

Chorus
Beautiful Ohio, where the golden grain
Dwarf the lovely flowers in the summer rain.
Cities rising high, silhouette the sky.
Freedom is supreme in this majestic land;
Mighty factories seem to hum in tune, so grand.
Beautiful Ohio, thy wonders are in view,
Land where my dreams all come true!

State Animal: White-Tailed Deer

Ohio named its largest **game animal**, the white-tailed deer, the official state animal in 1988. Eighty percent of Ohio's white-tailed deer herd lives in the hills of eastern Ohio. Because of overhunting and the destruction of their natural **habitat** by humans, the deer had disappeared in the state by 1904. That is just over 100 years after Ohio became a state. In 1923 with strict hunting laws in place, wildlife management officials brought deer back to Ohio. Today, you can find white-tailed deer in every one of Ohio's 88 counties.

The white-tailed deer is also the state animal of 11 other states.

The cardinal became Ohio's official state bird in 1933.

State Bird: Cardinal

One of the reasons Ohio's **legislature** chose the cardinal for the state bird is because it lives in Ohio throughout the year. The male is bright red with black eyes and markings around his beak. The female's drab feathers match the shades of the nest and tree branches so that she blends in with her surroundings.

State Insect: Ladybird Beetle

The ladybird beetle became Ohio's state insect in 1975. Most people know this insect by its common name—the ladybug. The legislature chose the insect because they thought it had attractive markings on its wings, and it helps to control harmful insect pests. The ladybird beetle eats garden and farm pests that destroy plants.

State Flower: Red Carnation

Ohio adopted the red carnation as its state flower in 1904. The Ohio legislature chose it as a way of honoring William McKinley, a U.S. president from Ohio. President McKinley kept a fresh bouquet of carnations on his desk and chose one to wear each day. He thought they brought him good luck. McKinley was **assassinated** in 1901 in Buffalo, New York. After that, Ohioans decided to make President McKinley's favorite flower a state symbol.

The carnation originally came from southern Europe.

State Beverage: Tomato Juice

Tomato juice became the official state beverage in 1965 when Ohio led the nation in producing the most tomato juice. Ohio does not grow as many tomatoes as California. However, it is the largest U.S. producer of processed tomato products.

State Tree: Buckeye

The buckeye tree became the official state tree in 1953. Long before Ohio adopted the tree as a state symbol, however, Ohioans called themselves Buckeyes, and Ohio was known as the Buckeye State. In 1839 when Ohioan William Henry Harrison campaigned for president of the United States, reporters picked up on his campaign symbol—the Ohio buckeye. The name stuck with Ohioans, and today people are called Buckeyes if they have Ohio roots.

The Ohio buckeye tree can grow up to 21 meters (69 feet) high.

Buckeyes

The word *buckeye* came from local Native Americans. Buckeye seeds have a round, brown shell with a pale spot that reminded them of the eye of a buck, or male deer. The Native American word for buckeye is *hetuck*.

State Fossil: Trilobite

The state **fossil** is the trilobite, a many-legged, sea-dwelling animal that lived around 440 million years ago. Trilobites lived in what is today Ohio when saltwater covered the land. The trilobite became Ohio's state fossil in 1985.

The Huffman Dam trilobite, found near Dayton, is about 37 centimeters (14.5 inches) long.

State Gemstone: Flint

Ohio adopted flint as its state gemstone in 1965. Flint is mined from the ground and is plentiful in central Ohio, around Newark. Ancient Native Americans living about 10,000 years ago first mined flint. They shaped such objects as weapons, knives, and other tools from it. Later, newcomers from Europe used flint to grind grains and to fire rifles. Today, flint—which comes in many colors and shades—is polished and used in jewelry.

State Reptile: Black Racer

Ohio's state reptile is the black racer snake. A fourth-grade student sent a letter to state representatives and senators suggesting that Ohio name an official reptile. He and his classmates decided on the black racer snake because it is native to all 88 Ohio counties and is called the farmer's friend. It eats mice and other rodents that destroy or eat crops.

The black racer snake has been a state symbol since 1995.

The bullfrog is named for its loud call.

State Amphibian: Bullfrog

In May 2002, the Ohio made the bullfrog—the state's largest frog— its official amphibian. Bullfrogs live all over Ohio.

State Motto

Ohio's state motto, "With God All Things Are Possible," was adopted in 1959. At that time, Ohio was the only state in the country without a motto. In 2001 people began to question whether the motto was proper because it is a phrase from the Bible and contains the word *God*. People who did not like the motto felt that Ohio was breaking laws separating religion and government. A judge decided that the motto was legal, as long as the Bible was not **cited** with the motto.

State Quarter

The Ohio quarter, the 17th in the 50 State Quarters Program (Ohio was the 17th state to enter the Union), became available in 2002. The quarter celebrates Ohio's role in **aviation** and space travel. In the early 1900s, the Wright brothers lived in Dayton and built and flew the first airplane. On July 20, 1969, Neil Armstrong of Wapakoneta was the first person to walk on the moon. On February 20, 1962, John Glenn of New Concord was the first person to circle the Earth. On October 29, 1998, at age 77, he became the oldest person to travel in space.

The quarter contains an astronaut and the Wright brothers' early plane.

Ohio's Government

Like the federal government, Ohio's state government has three main branches. The **legislative** branch makes the laws. The **executive** branch carries out the laws. The **judicial** branch **enforces** the laws and decides how to apply them.

The Legislative Branch

The state legislative branch makes state laws. The people who work in this part of government are elected leaders called senators or representatives. Ohio is divided into voting districts based upon population. There are a total of 132 districts—99 for choosing representatives and 33 for choosing senators. Voters are citizens 18 years of age and older. Each district elects a senator or representative to work in Columbus, the state capital.

Ohio Governor Ted Strickland gives a speech to the people of the state. As governor, he is a member of the executive branch of Ohio's government.

Executive Branch

Governor
(four-year term)

Carries out the laws
of the state

Legislative Branch

Ohio Legislature

33 State Senators (four-year term)	99 State Representatives (two-year term)

Makes laws

Judicial Branch

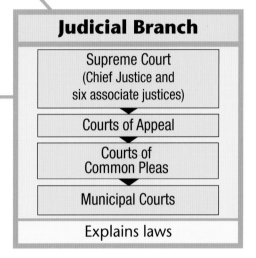

Supreme Court
(Chief Justice and
six associate justices)

▼

Courts of Appeal

▼

Courts of
Common Pleas

▼

Municipal Courts

Explains laws

The organization of Ohio's state government is similar to that of the U.S. government.

Voters elect the 99 members of the Ohio House of Representatives to a **term** of two years. Representatives cannot serve more than four terms in a row. The 33 Ohio senators are elected to a term of four years. Senators cannot serve more than two terms in a row. Both decide whether **bills** brought before them should become laws. Once the House and the Senate—together called the Ohio General Assembly—pass a bill, it must be signed by the governor to become law.

The governor then either signs or **vetoes** the bill. If the governor does nothing, after ten days the bill becomes a law. When the governor vetoes a bill, it is sent back to the General Assembly for changes. It can also become a law if three-fifths of the legislators vote to override, or vote against, the governor. Passed laws are called the Ohio Revised Code.

Governor Ted Strickland greets voters at Central State University in Ohio.

The Executive Branch

Like the federal government, in which the president is the leader of the entire country, the governor is the leader of his or her state. The governor of Ohio can be reelected for a total of two terms of four years each. The governor's **cabinet** is made up of the heads of each state department. Ohio has more than 20 departments, including the Department of Natural Resources and the Department of Health.

After the Ohio General Assembly passes bills, the governor signs them into law. The governor also has other responsibilities, such as preparing the state budget.

The executive branch includes other elected officials. The secretary of state oversees the county election boards, keeps track of Ohio businesses, and records all the laws that are passed. The Ohio lieutenant governor takes over for the governor when necessary. The state treasurer manages state money, and the state auditor makes sure there are no mistakes in the way money is handled by these offices. The attorney general represents the state in all state-related law trials.

The Judicial Branch

The judicial branch of government enforces the laws and decides how to apply them in real situations. These decisions are usually made in courts of law.

In Ohio, there are three levels of law courts—municipal courts, county courts, **appellate** courts, and the supreme court. Only county court trials may move into the appellate or supreme court level. Cases that are more serious are first heard in a county court. Not all counties have the same number of courts. County courts are called courts of common pleas. Less serious cases are heard in municipal courts.

The county court findings may be **appealed** to a higher court. Ohio has 12 appellate districts. Each has an appellate court and several judges, depending upon how large and busy the district is.

When the appellate court fails to settle a case, it is taken to the Ohio Supreme Court, the highest court in the state. Ohio's supreme court justices, as well as other Ohio justices, are elected and serve a term of six years.

Ohio has seven supreme court judges. Pictured in the front-center is Thomas J. Moyer, Ohio's chief justice since 1987.

Working in Ohio's Government

The three branches of Ohio's state government work in the Capitol Square or in buildings that are nearby in downtown Columbus. The capitol building was restored and looks similar to the original, built in 1861. The capitol's unique design is nicknamed the "hat box" because its flat, round roof resembles the shape of box used to store fancy hats. The ceiling of the capitol's **rotunda** is an 8.8-meter- (29-foot-) wide skylight. The center circle of the skylight is a hand-painted seal of Ohio. Most other state capitols, including the U.S. Capitol, have a dome design.

Outside the building, cannons used in the Civil War (1861–1865) and statues encircle the capitol. Behind the building, Ohio **Veterans'** Plaza honors all of Ohio's veterans. The plaza consists of two curved limestone walls, 3 meters (10 feet) high and 12 meters (40 feet) long. Letters soldiers wrote to loved ones back home are engraved in limestone and surrounded by state flags.

The floor of the capitol's rotunda consists of nearly 5,000 pieces of handcut marble from around the world.

Local Government

Cities in Ohio follow the plans set by the city or town **charter**. The charter outlines each city's geographic borders and explains the type of government the city or village follows.

One example of an Ohio city government is Dayton. Since 1913 the mayor and four **commissioners** have run the city government. Voters elect them to terms of four years. This group then appoints a city manager. The city manager has two assistant city managers and one **deputy** city manager. Together, they are responsible for carrying out city plans and rules and giving direction to the various departments within Dayton. Two of the departments include the Department of **Aviation** and the Department of Fire.

Mansfield, a city of about 50,000 residents in north-central Ohio, has a different type of government than Dayton. Mansfield's type of government is called a mayor-**council** plan. The mayor and city council work together to run the city government. Voters elect the Mansfield mayor to a term of four years. She or he can serve a total of three terms.

The city of Dayton renovated its city hall in 1997.

Birthplace of Presidents

William Henry Harrison

William Henry Harrison (1773–1841) was the only Ohio president not born in the state. He served only 31 days in office. He died of pneumonia. He holds the record for the president with the shortest **term** of office.

Ulysses S. Grant

Ulysses S. Grant (1822–1885) commanded the Union army during the Civil War (1861–1865). His first term saw the passage of the 15th Amendment to the Constitution in 1870. It said that voting rights could not be denied to a person based on race or color.

Ulysses S. Grant was born in this home in Point Pleasant, Ohio.

Rutherford B. Hayes

Rutherford B. Hayes (1822–1893) won the disputed election of 1876 by one **electoral vote**. The result was assured by a dishonest election **commission** with a majority of Southerners. Hayes's wife was the first president's wife to be called First Lady.

Rutherford B. Hayes grew up in this house in Fremont, Ohio.

Ohio's Presidents

Name	Birthplace	Term	Order
William Henry Harrison	Berkeley, Va.	1841	9th
Ulysses S. Grant	Point Pleasant, Oh.	1869–1877	18th
Rutherford B. Hayes	Delaware, Oh.	1877–1881	19th
James Garfield	Orange, Oh.	1881	20th
Benjamin Harrison	North Bend, Oh.	1889–1893	23rd
William McKinley	Niles, Oh.	1897–1901	25th
William Howard Taft	Cincinnati, Oh.	1909–1913	27th
Warren G. Harding	Blooming Grove, Oh.	1921–1923	29th

James Garfield

James Garfield (1831–1881) grew up in poverty. He helped support his family with many jobs, including working on the Ohio Canal. Garfield served only four months as president. A mentally disturbed person **assassinated** him. Garfield did not die directly from the gunshot wound. Instead, infections from unclean health practices of the time caused his death four months later.

Benjamin Harrison

Benjamin Harrison (1833–1901) was the grandson of William Henry Harrison. In the election of 1888, Harrison won the presidency with fewer **popular votes** than his opponent—just as George W. Bush did in the 2000 election.

William McKinley

William McKinley (1843–1901) was president when the United States fought and won the Spanish-American War (1898). McKinley was elected to a second term but was assassinated a few months after his reelection. During a ceremony in 1901, he bent down to give the red carnation he was wearing to a young girl. At that moment, a gunman's bullet struck him. He died eight days later.

This house in Cincinnati was the home of William Howard Taft.

William Howard Taft

William Howard Taft (1857–1930) became the first president to throw out the season's first pitch to start the professional baseball season. Taft was the only president to serve as a chief justice of the U.S. Supreme Court. Taft's wife, as first lady, also arranged the planting of the pink Japanese cherry blossoms that now bloom throughout Washington, D.C., each spring.

Warren G. Harding

Warren G. Harding's (1865–1923) election marked the first time that women voted. He won the election by a wide margin. Unfortunately, his term was marked by many acts of poor conduct and widespread dishonesty in government. He died while he was still in office.

Culture in Ohio

Ohio's art and music lovers find many cultural activities and attractions throughout the state.

Music

The Cincinnati Symphony Orchestra, playing since 1895, is the fifth oldest orchestra in the United States. Cincinnati historians say musical groups formed and played in Cincinnati long before—as early as 1825. The Cincinnati Symphony has been home to the U.S. **premieres** of works by such composers as Claude Debussy (1862–1918), Maurice Ravel (1875–1937), and Béla Bartók (1881–1945). It has also **commissioned** famous American works such as John Copland's "Fanfare for the Common Man." The Cleveland Orchestra, founded in 1918, performs at Severance Center in the University Circle area of Cleveland. During the summer, it plays outdoors at Blossom Music Center in Akron.

The Columbus Symphony Orchestra performs above.

Art

Ohio has a large number of art museums. Founded in 1919, the Butler Institute of American Art in Youngstown was the first place in the United States built especially to show a collection of American art. Unlike most other art galleries, it is okay to touch the exhibits in Butler's Sweeney Children's Gallery. In addition, the Donnell Gallery of the Butler Institute features paintings, sculptures, and drawings with sports themes. It is the only museum gallery of its kind in the United States.

The Cincinnati Art Museum first opened in 1881, making it the first art museum west of the **Allegheny Mountains** to have its own building. Today, it has 88 galleries and more than 80,000 works from all over the world in its permanent collection. The collections in this museum include art from the present day to ancient Greece, Rome, and Egypt—thousands of years of art history.

Greeting from Ohio

Stamps are a popular form of art. In April 2002, the U.S. Postal Service released a set of "Greetings from America" stamps. They were released at ceremonies held in every state on the same day. The stamps celebrate the uniqueness of each of the 50 states. The Ohio stamp features Cleveland and some of the tall buildings of the city's skyline.

Theater

You can find comedy, opera, musicals, or dance productions throughout Ohio. The Cleveland Play House is the oldest **resident** theater company in the United States. It has presented plays since 1915. In addition, Ohio has many other professional and children's theaters and more than 100 community theaters. Many college performances help students learn and provide excellent entertainment for theater lovers.

Ohio's Schools

Education is a large part of Ohio's culture, too. The first schools in Ohio were established in the 1700s, long before it became a state.

- German immigrants started the first U.S. school with a kindergarten class in 1838 near German Village.

- Columbus Public Schools opened the first U.S. junior high school—Indianola Junior High School—in 1909.

- Ohio University in Athens, Ohio's first college, opened in 1804.

- In 1833 Oberlin College opened as the first **interracial/coeducational** college in the United States.

In 1841 Oberlin, pictured below, gave three women bachelor's degrees—the first women in the United States to receive college degrees.

Ohio's Farm Festivals

Two boys show off their prize pumpkin at the Circleville Pumpkin Festival.

Festivals throughout the year celebrate Ohio's strong farming heritage. About 80,000 farms in Ohio supply residents and people of other states with farm-fresh products. In addition, farming provides millions of dollars to Ohio's economy each year.

Circleville Pumpkin Festival

The Circleville Pumpkin Festival was started in 1903. It is Ohio's oldest and largest festival. Today, more than 300,000 people visit the festival. Each year a prize is given for the largest pumpkin. In 2007 the prize went to a record-setting pumpkin weighing 691.5 kilograms (1,524.5 pounds)!

Corn Festival in Millersport

The Sweet Corn Festival in Millersport has been held each year since 1947. In that year, one kettle was needed to boil the corn for the festival. Today, several 7,571-liter (2,000-gallon) vats are needed to make corn for festival-goers. This festival also features a corn-eating contest and an outhouse race. Three person teams, with two pushing and one riding inside, move an outhouse on wheels about 12 meters (40 feet), circle a marker, and return to the starting line while being timed.

Ohio has about 37,000 corn farms and is the sixth largest corn-producing state.

Ohio's Festivals

There are plenty of other festivals that celebrate Ohio's farming heritage. Here are the names of just a few:

American Soya Festival, Amanda
Applebutter Stirrin' Festival, Coshocton
Bratwurst Festival, Bucyrus
Dandelion May Fest, Dover
Grape Jamboree, Geneva
Maple Sugar Weekends, Burton
Melon Festival, Milan
Ohio Gourd Festival, Mount Gilead
Ohio Honey Festival, Hamilton

Ohio Sauerkraut Festival, Waynesville
Ohio Swiss Festival, Sugarcreek
Popcorn Festival, Marion
Potato Festival, Mantua
Raspberry Festival, Urbana
Strawberry Festival, Troy
Tomato Festival, Reynoldsburg
Utica Old Fashioned Ice Cream Festival, Utica
Zucchinifest, Obetz

Ohio's Food

For a taste of Ohio's food, many Ohioans go to one of the many food **festivals** around the state. The Taste of Cincinnati, which began in 1979, is the nation's longest-running food festival. More than 500,000 people go to the Taste of Cincinnati, which features more than 40 restaurants serving up many of their menu items.

Skyline Chili

Many people in Cincinnati consider Skyline Chili to have the city's best chili. Nicholas Lambrinides, a Greek immigrant, started the restaurant in 1949 after his arrival in the United States. Lambrinides named his restaurant Skyline Chili because he could see the Cincinnati skyline from the restaurant's kitchen. Today, all chili at Skyline, which has more than 100 locations, is still made from Lambrinides's secret recipe. It is kept in a safe and is known only to a few.

Cincinnati Chili

One of the unique dishes at the Taste of Cincinnati is Cincinnati-style chili. Much different from traditional, or Texas-style, chili, Cincinnati chili is more like a topping. It is flavored with cinnamon and unsweetened chocolate. People put it on hot dogs or spaghetti, making what people in Cincinnati call the Three-Way. In Cincinnati, true chili-eaters have their chili one of five ways:

- Plain

- Two-Way—spaghetti and chili

- Three-Way—chili, spaghetti, and cheddar cheese

- Four-Way—chili, spaghetti, cheddar cheese, and onions

- Five-Way—chili, spaghetti, cheddar cheese, onions and kidney beans

Ohio Buckeyes

If you want something sweet, try some Ohio buckeyes:

- 1 16–18-oz jar creamy peanut butter
- 4 cups powdered sugar
- 1 cup (2 sticks) soft butter or margarine (leave at room temperature for an hour or two to soften)
- 1 12-oz bag chocolate chips
- 1/2 cake paraffin wax

Always make sure to have an adult work the stove for you!

1. Combine peanut butter, sugar, and softened butter/margarine in very large bowl. Mix well, and roll into small balls about one inch in diameter. If balls are soft after shaping, refrigerate until firm.

2. Melt chocolate and paraffin together in double boiler or in small, deep bowl in the microwave.

3. Use a toothpick or bamboo skewer to dip peanut butter balls in melted chocolate, leaving the very top of balls without chocolate to look like a real buckeye. Set buckeyes on cookie sheets lined with waxed paper and let cool.

Ohio's Folklore and Legends

The words *folklore* and *folktales* describe stories that are told by one **generation** to the next over many years. The stories explain why something is done or explain how something started. They can also teach a lesson about life.

Shawnee Creation Myth

The Shawnee are a Native American people that lived in what is today Ohio. The Shawnee have their own story of their people's creation.

The legend says that the Shawnee began in a different world—an island balanced on the back of a giant turtle. According to Shawnee myth, when the first people were on the island, they could see nothing but water. They did not know how to cross it. They prayed for help, and one day they were carried across the water.

Native Americans gather corn during the fall harvest.

The Shawnees are unique among Native American peoples in that their creator was a woman. They called this person Kokumthena, which means Our Grandmother. Kokumthena is usually shown with gray hair. In pictures her size ranges from huge to small. According to Shawnee myth, the idea of creation came from the Supreme Being, who was called Moneto. However, Kokumthena did the actual work. As a result, she is the most important figure in Shawnee religion.

Delaware Animal Lesson

While some Native American folktales focus on creation and tribal history, other stories focus on teaching children life lessons. Some lessons teach the young Delaware, for example, to be thankful for food and to respect nature.

One story from Ohio's Delaware people tells of a young boy who shoots and wounds a bear. However, he does not shoot it for food. The Delaware look upon that act as torturing the animal. Soon, the other bears in the forest begin to punish the boy. They tear off his arms and legs, put them back on, and let him run home. Upon reaching his village, his arms and legs fall off.

This story teaches children that failing to treat animals with respect is wrong. Today's native peoples continue to have strong beliefs about respecting their environment.

Ohio's Sports

Ohio has a long history of both professional and college sports. Ohio has eight major professional teams and many college sports teams, too.

Cleveland Sports

Head to Cleveland to catch Major League Baseball's (MLB) Indians or the National Football league's (NFL) Browns. The Indians, which began play in 1901, have enjoyed recent success. They have won seven division titles and two American League titles between 1994 and 2008. In 1946 the Browns began play. They have won four NFL championships and boast 20 NFL Hall of Famers, including Jim Brown, widely considered the greatest running back in NFL history.

Another Cleveland team—the Rockers of the Women's National Basketball Association (WNBA)—began play in 1997. They made the WNBA playoffs in 1998, 2000, and 2001.

The Cleveland Indians began playing at Jacob's Field in 1994.

NFL Footballs and Whistles

NFL teams around the country get their footballs and their whistles from Ohio. The Wilson Company, in Ada, the only manufacturer of leather footballs in the United States, supplies the footballs used in NFL play. The metal whistles used by the NFL are also made in Ohio, at the American Whistle Corporation, in Columbus.

Cincinnati Baseball

The Cincinnati Reds, originally called the Red Stockings, are the oldest professional baseball team in the country. They began play in 1869 and in that year completed the longest winning streak in baseball history. Their final official record was 57-0. Their streak continued into 1870, when it ended at 81 games at the hands of the Brooklyn Atlantics. The Reds have won the World Series five times and now play in the Great American Ballpark, which opened in 2003.

Columbus Sports

In Columbus, professional soccer has taken hold with Major League Soccer's Columbus Crew. In 1994 newly formed Major League Soccer awarded Columbus with one of its ten clubs. The Crew made it to the conference finals three years in a row between 1997 and 1999 and won a title in 2008. They play in a state-of-the-art stadium designed for soccer only. Crew Stadium opened in 1999.

A Miami defender hauls down Ohio State's Chris Gamble after a 56-yard catch in the Buckeyes' 2003 Fiesta Bowl victory.

Ohioans love college sports, too—especially teams from the Ohio State University in Columbus. The Ohio State Buckeyes have won 30 national championships in a variety of sports, including seven in football, with their most recent one in the 2006 Fiesta Bowl. The Buckeyes also have 11 national championships in men's swimming and diving.

Lords and Ladies of Kenyon

Kenyon College, in Gambier, Ohio, has won every men's swimming and diving NCAA Division III national championship from 1980 to 2008. It is the only team in the history of the NCAA to win 28 straight national championships—in any sport and any division. In addition, Kenyon has won every women's swimming and diving NCAA Division III national championship from 1984 to 2008—that is 22 in a row. Jim Steen, the Kenyon coach since 1975, has led the school to all 50 of its swimming and diving national championships.

Ohio's Businesses and Products

Ohio is home to some of the world's leading industrial companies, including many food production companies and **vehicle** manufacturing plants.

The Food Industry

Ohio's food industry produced $25.2 billion worth of goods in 2006, ranking it 18th in agricultural production in the nation. One major reason for Ohio's leading position in this area is the state's location—between the grain belt in the Midwest and the population centers in the East. Ohio is located within 805 kilometers (500 miles) of 60 percent of the nation's population, including the population centers of Canada. The distance of 805 kilometers (500 miles) is important because it is about a day's drive for the trucks that ship these goods.

Some major food companies are headquartered in Ohio, including the J. M. Smucker company. It makes jams, jellies, and peanut butter. The Bob Evans Farms company, which makes such foods as breakfast sausages, is located in Columbus. Wendy's International, the fast-food restaurant chain, is located in Dublin.

Smuckers has its headquarters here, in Orrville, Ohio.

This General Mills plant, in Wellston, helps make Ohio one of the nation's leading shippers of frozen specialty foods.

However, the real strength behind Ohio's food industry lies in its manufacturing plants.

- Campbell's operates the world's largest soup factory, in Napoleon. It produces about 90 million cases of soup and juice products per day.

- General Mills runs the world's largest pizza plant, in Wellston. It turns out about 1.2 million pizzas per day.

- Heinz runs a plant in Fremont that makes more ketchup than anywhere else in the world. It produces more than 8.4 million restaurant-sized bottles per year.

- Dannon owns the world's largest yogurt plant, in Minster. It produces about 230,000 cups of yogurt an hour—that is about 3 million cups per day.

Vehicle Manufacturing

Ohio is also home to many automobile factories, including one of the country's largest manufacturing centers, in Lordstown, near Cleveland. Lordstown Assembly and the Lordstown Metal Center employ more than 6,000 people combined. Lordstown Assembly opened in 1966, and the Lordstown Metal Center opened in 1969.

The Lordstown Metal Center, which is about 2.5 million square meters (2.7 million square feet), is a metal production plant.

In 1979 Marysville became the center of Japanese **vehicle** manufacturing. Honda opened its first U.S. factory with the Marysville Motorcycle Plant. This plant can produce up to 150,000 motorcycles per year. Three years later, in 1982, Honda opened the Marysville Auto plant. The 3.3 million-square-meter (3.5 million-square-foot) plant can produce up to 440,000 cars per year and employs more than 5,000 people.

The Marysville Auto Plant has the highest output of any single auto plant in the United States.

Ohio's Attractions and Landmarks

Look at the map of Ohio on page 5 again. You will find that Ohio is full of activities and attractions for everyone.

Attractions

One of the world's most famous amusement parks is Cedar Point, located on the shores of Lake Erie, in Sandusky. Cedar Point, which opened in 1870, now operates 17 roller coasters, more than any other park in world. In 2003 it also opened the tallest and fastest roller coaster in the world. Named the Top Thrill Dragster, the ride's first tower is 128 meters (420 feet) high, and the cars travel at a top speed of 193 kilometers per hour (120 miles per hour).

Next on your list might be zoos, and Ohio has many choices. One of the oldest zoos in the country, the Cleveland Metroparks Zoo, opened in 1882. It has the largest number of **primates** in North America and has other animals from all over the world, from a South American armadillo to an African zebra. You can also stroll through different rain forests.

Visitors to Cedar Point enjoy riding one of the park's many roller coasters.

Halls of Fame

If you love sports, then head to Canton, home of the Professional Football Hall of Fame. It opened in 1963 and tells the history of professional football. You can learn about the game's great players, such as Walter Payton and Joe Montana, and you can learn how the game has changed. You can also see famous NFL players' equipment in the Moments, Memories & Mementos Gallery.

Football equipment from the 1920s to the present is on display at the Pro Football Hall of Fame.

Find out all about the invention of ice cream at the National Inventors Hall of Fame, in Akron. It gives everyone a chance to create an invention and learn about past inventors and inventions. Ohio's own famous inventors, such as Thomas Edison, Garrett Morgan, and Charles Kettering, are featured there. In addition, the museum celebrates more than 150 of the men and women whose inventions changed the United States.

The National Inventors Hall of Fame opened in 1973.

Another unique Ohio landmark is the Rock and Roll Hall of Fame, which opened in 1995 in Cleveland. Cleveland's ties to the birth of rock and roll are strong. In 1951 Cleveland disc jockey Alan Freed was the first to use the expression *rock and roll*. In addition, Cleveland has seen the early success of such rock and roll pioneers as Chuck Berry and Elvis Presley. You can also learn about famous bands such as the Rolling Stones and see some of their actual instruments.

Air and Space

Ohio has a rich history in **aviation** and space exploration. In Dayton you can stop at the Wright Cycle Shop, now a national historical park, to see the original 1905 Wright Flyer III. The Wright brothers invented the world's first airplane able to stay in the air for more than a few seconds. Also in Dayton is the U.S. Air Force Museum, the world's largest and oldest military aviation museum. The museum contains hundreds of aircraft and other exhibits. They include an F117A Stealth Bomber, the presidents' old Boeing 707, and a German Fokker Dr.I triplane. The Red Baron, Germany's famous flying ace, flew the Fokker Dr.I in World War I (1914–1918).

The Wright brothers made their own line of bicycles in the late 1800s—some of which are in the Wright Cycle Shop.

More than one million people visit the U.S. Air Force Museum each year.

History

For those interested in history, Ohio has many museums and activities. The National Underground Railroad Freedom Center, in Cincinnati, opened in August 2004. It gives the history of the African American struggle for freedom. Ohio also played a large role in the Underground Railroad. It was a secret system of helping slaves move through Ohio toward freedom before the Civil War ended slavery in the United States in 1865. Those who helped slaves were nicknamed conductors. Their safe homes were called stops. There are dozens and dozens of stops still standing, including John Rankin's house, in Ripley. He and his wife helped thousands of slaves toward freedom.

From 1825 to 1865, Rankin sheltered escaping slaves in his house, in Ripley.

A boy learns the art of basket weaving at Ohio Village.

Ohio also has something called living history museums. Here, costumed guides take you back to earlier times with hands-on demonstrations and activities. One such place is Ohio Village, in Columbus, where they teach about life before the Civil War (1861–1865).

You can see where children of the time went to school, which was open every day of the year except Sundays and Christmas Day. There were no holidays or vacation days. Then check out a typical farmhouse. You can even pitch in and help wash dishes and do the laundry. Everything had to be done by hand, without the help of dishwashers and laundry machines.

Historical Sites

Ohio has a large collection of prehistoric Native American mounds dating back more than 1,000 years. One such mound—Fort Ancient, near Lebanon—is the largest hilltop earth structure in the United States. Its walls rise more than 6 meters (20 feet) high and are about 5 kilometers (3 miles) long. They enclose an area of about 40.5 hectares (100 acres).

One of the world's most famous prehistoric mounds is near Hillsboro. It is called the Great Serpent Mound because its shape looks like a snake. The mound has 7 curves, rises to a height of over 1.2 meters (4 feet), and stretches more than 0.4 kilometer (0.25 mile). The purpose of the mound is unknown.

The Adena peoples built the Great Serpent Mound.

Ohio's Bridges, Structures, and Ships

Ohio ranks 35th among all the states in size, but it is second only to Texas in the number of bridges. In addition, Cleveland is home to two of the world's tallest buildings—Key Tower and Terminal Tower.

Ohio's Famous Bridges

The Roebling Suspension Bridge connects Cincinnati with Covington, Kentucky. It was the longest **suspension bridge** in the world at the time it was built. The technology for such a long bridge did not exist until engineer John Roebling made plans for the bridge.

The Roebling Suspension Bridge opened in 1866.

The Harpersfield Bridge was originally built in 1868.

Ohio is also famous for its covered bridges. In the 1800s, Ohio had more than 3,000 covered bridges. About 135 of these wooden covered bridges are left. The longest covered bridge in Ohio is 69.5 meters (228 feet) long. This is the Harpersfield Bridge, which crosses the Grand River in Ashtabula County.

Terminal Tower and Key Tower

From 1930 until 1967, Terminal Tower was the tallest building in the world outside of New York City. The tower, completed in 1930, has a 19-meter- (63-foot-) tall flagpole. The tower and the flagpole together make the building 235 meters (771 feet) tall. Terminal Tower's steel-reinforced concrete support pillars reach more than 76 meters (250 feet) below the ground.

Key Tower in Cleveland towers 290 meters (950 feet) over the streets of the city. It is the tallest building between Chicago and New York City.

Terminal Tower rises above the Cleveland skyline.

Ohio's Ships

Ohio has had many ships named after it. The first USS *Ohio*, a merchant ship, was bought by the navy in 1812. The navy changed it into a warship and put it into service in 1813. The ship served on Lake Erie during the War of 1812 in a squadron commanded by Commodore Oliver H. Perry.

The current USS *Ohio* is a nuclear-powered submarine. After several sea trials, the U.S. Navy accepted the ship in 1981. Since then, the navy has upgraded the USS *Ohio* with new equipment, and it has completed more than 60 patrols throughout the world. Originally, the USS *Ohio* was set to retire in 2002, but instead it has been equipped with the most modern weapons and will help protect the United States well into the 2000s.

The USS *Ohio* cruises through its trials in 1981.

Map of Ohio

Lake Erie

Toledo
Napoleon
Cleveland
Orange
Sandusky
Oberlin
Niles
Fremont
Lordstown
Youngstown
Akron
Maumee River
Sandusky River
Cuyahoga R.
Ohio City
Ada
Mansfield
Orrville
Canton
Grand Lake
Wapakoneta
Delaware Lake
Gambier
Marysville
Quincy
Delaware
Minster
Dublin
Scioto River
Zanesville
Columbus
New Concord
Quaker City
New Carlisle
Millersport
Muskingum River
Dayton
Xenia
Circleville
Lebanon
Great Miami River
Athens
North Bend
Hillsboro
Zaleski
Cincinnati
Point Pleasant
Wellston
Ripley
Ohio River
Ohio River

N
W   E
S

| 0 | 50 miles |
| 0 | 50 km |

⊙	Capital
•	City
～	River
—	State line

Wisconsin
Michigan
Pennsylvania
Illinois
Indiana
Ohio
Delaware
West Virginia
Kentucky
Virginia

Glossary

Allegheny Mountains a mountain range that runs through Ohio and several other states in the eastern United States

appeal to ask a higher court to review a lower court's decision

appellate word that describes a court that reviews decisions made by lower courts

assassinate to kill someone for political reasons

aviation anything that has to do with airplanes or other aircraft

bills what state laws are called before they are actually passed by the legislature

cabinet a group of leaders that helps a governor run the state government

charter a written description of the boundaries, government, and powers of a city

cite to refer to or to mention formally

coeducational word that describes a school that has both male and female students

commissioned hired by an organization to create a new piece of art. Music composers, writers, sculptors, and other types of artists are often commissioned to create works.

commissioners/commission people who are in charge of departments or offices in city government. A commission is a group of such people.

council a group of elected lawmakers

deputy a person who acts as second in command to an elected official

electoral vote a vote that is cast by a member of a group that is specially chosen to elect a high official. The U.S. president is elected by a group called the electoral college.

enforces makes sure that people obey the law

executive word that describes something that has to do with enforcing laws for a state or country

festival special celebration that includes food, cultural events, and entertainment

fossil the remains of an ancient living thing. Most fossils are remains that have turned to stone or whose outlines have been preserved in stone.

game animal animal that is hunted for sport or food

generation the average span of time between parents and their children—about 20 to 25 years

habitat place where a plant or animal lives

interracial word that describes a school or other organization that includes people of all races

judicial word that describes something that has to do with the court system of a state or country

legislative word that describes something that has to do with lawmaking for a state or country

legislature group of people who are elected to make laws for a state or country

Northwest Territory a huge area of what is now the United States. It included what are now the states of Ohio, Indiana, Illinois, Michigan, Wisconsin, and part of Minnesota.

popular votes votes cast directly by the citizens

premiere very first performance of a new piece of music, play, movie, or other form of entertainment

primates monkeys, apes, and related animals

resident word that describes a group, such as a theater company, that stays in one location permanently

rotunda large, round room

suspension bridge type of bridge that hangs from cables that are supported by towers

term set period during which an elected official serves

vehicle something that can be driven, such as a car, motorcycle, bus, or truck

veteran a person who has served in the armed forces during a war

veto to forbid or prevent

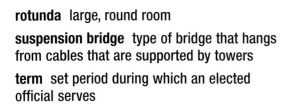

Find Out More

Books

Brown, Jonathan A. and Frances Ruffin. *Ohio*. Strongsville, OH: Gareth Stevens, 2006.

Curry, Judson and Elizabeth Curry. *Regions of the USA: The Midwest*. Chicago: Raintree, 2007.

Gregson, Susan R. *Tecumseh: Shawnee Leader*. Mankato, MN: Capstone Press, 2003.

Hart, Joyce. *It's My State! Ohio*. Tarrytown, NY: Marshall Cavendish, 2006.

McAuliffe, Emily. *Ohio Facts and Symbols*. Mankato, MN: Capstone Press, 2003.

Schonberg, Marcia. *People of Ohio.* Chicago: Heinemann Library, 2009.

Websites

http://ohio.gov/

Ohio's state government provides this helpful and link-filled site. It lists information about the state's animals, flag, parks, and more.

http://ohsweb.ohiohistory.org/places/index.shtml

Learn more about the history of Ohio at this site, sponsored by the Ohio Historical Society.

http://www.profootballhof.com/

The Pro Football Hall of Fame in Canton, Ohio, provides this website filled with facts about famous NFL players, teams, and coaches.

Index